COACHING AND COUNSELING

A Practical Guide for Managers and Team Leaders

Revised

Marianne Minor

A FIFTY-MINUTE™ SERIES BOOK

CRISP PUBLICATIONS, INC.
Menlo Park, California

COACHING AND COUNSELING
A Practical Guide for Managers and Team Leaders

Revised

by Marianne Minor

CREDITS:
Editor: **Michael G. Crisp**
Typesetting: **Interface Studio**
Cover Design: **Carol Harris**
Artwork: **Ralph Mapson**

Copyright © 1989, 1996 by Crisp Publications, Inc.
Printed in the United States of America.

Distribution to the U.S. Trade:

National Book Network, Inc.
4720 Boston Way
Lanham, MD 20706
1-800-462-6420

Library of Congress Catalog Card Number 95-83501
Minor, Marianne
Coaching and Counseling—Revised
ISBN 1-56052-386-7

This book is printed on recyclable paper with soy ink.

LEARNING OBJECTIVES FOR:

COACHING AND COUNSELING— REVISED EDITION

The objectives for *Coaching and Counseling—Revised Edition* are listed below. They have been developed to guide you, the reader, to the core issues covered in this book.

Objectives

❑ 1) To explain how to teach both job skills and counseling

❑ 2) To help decide whether to coach or counsel

❑ 3) To suggest ways to give effective feedback

❑ 4) To help translate the principles of coaching or counseling into action

Assessing Your Progress

In addition to the Learning Objectives, Crisp, Inc. has developed an **assessment** that covers the fundamental information presented in this book. A twenty-five item, multiple choice/true-false questionnaire allows the reader to evaluate his or her comprehension of the subject matter. An answer sheet with a summary matching the questions to the listed objectives, is also available. To learn how to obtain a copy of this assessment please call: **1-800-442-7477** and ask to speak with a Customer Service Representative.

DEDICATION

This book is dedicated to my husband, Gregory C. Paraskou,
who confirmed my suspicion that I could do whatever
I set out to do. His belief in doing work that you love helped
me take risks and build a thriving business that I love.

Marianne Minor

Marianne Minor

ABOUT THE AUTHOR

Marianne Minor is a licensed clinical social worker and management consultant. She has taught management and leadership programs internationally for Fortune 500 companies. She has also taught in graduate management programs at San Jose State University and the University of San Francisco.

She has designed and conducted numerous training programs for high-tech manufacturing and utility companies. Marianne has consulted with school districts on how to implement human resource systems and decentralized decision making. She specializes in team building and leadership programs.

She is president of her own consulting firm, Marianne Minor and Associates, in Silicon Valley, California.

The author may be contacted through Crisp Publications.

ABOUT THE SERIES

With over 200 titles in print, the acclaimed Crisp 50-Minute™ series presents self-paced learning at its easiest and best. These comprehensive self-study books for business or personal use are filled with exercises, activities, assessments, and case studies that capture your interest and increase your understanding.

Other Crisp products, based on the 50-Minute books, are available in a variety of learning style formats for both individual and group study, including audio, video, CD-ROM, and computer-based training.

PREFACE

This book is for anyone who wants to influence, direct, teach or motivate others, either formally as a manager or supervisor; or informally as a team leader, or team member.

Counseling and coaching are skills that can be learned through persistence and patience. If you have a sincere desire to develop and support others and the self-discipline to practice the specific strategies, you can become proficient in these areas.

The rewards from improving your counseling and coaching skills are many. You can use these skills to create optimal working conditions which include: proper orientation and training for employees, establishing clear responsibilities and standards, providing appropriate guidance and support during times of transition and insuring increased motivation and productivity through effective feedback.

This book will enable you to analyze and develop your coaching and counseling skills. The emphasis will be on how these skills affect the workplace. After you complete this book you will know practical guidelines and specific strategies to assist others in dealing with their personal problems and motivating employees to improve performance on the job.

CONTENTS

SECTION

I

Counseling and Coaching

THE WHAT AND WHY OF COUNSELING AND COACHING

By the end of this section you should have a clear idea of what counseling and coaching are and what skills they require. You will also have a good idea of how effective you are as a counselor or coach.

In order to get to this endpoint you will answer quizzes and appraise your own skills.

But first let's start with the basics.

DEFINITIONS AHEAD

DEFINITIONS OF COUNSELING AND COACHING

Counseling: A supportive process by a manager to help an employee define and work through personal problems or organizational changes that affect job performance.

Coaching: A directive process by a manager to train and orient an employee to the realities of the workplace and to help the employee remove barriers to optimum work performance.

Counseling and coaching share many of the same skills. At times they may seem to overlap. When they do, remember the following diagrams. These diagrams (shown below) will help you differentiate the two processes.

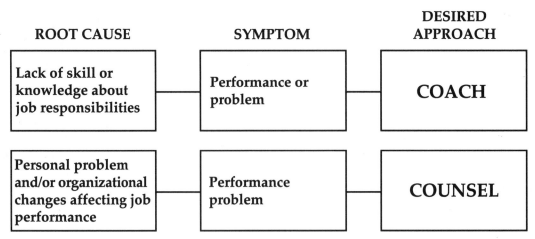

ROOT CAUSE	SYMPTOM	DESIRED APPROACH
Lack of skill or knowledge about job responsibilities	Performance or problem	COACH
Personal problem and/or organizational changes affecting job performance	Performance problem	COUNSEL

THE BENEFITS OF COUNSELING

Let's face it. Most of us need to see a personal payoff before we change our behavior. The same holds true for deciding to become the best possible coach or counselor you can.

Why should you improve your counseling skills? Read each of the following statements below. Do you think they are true or false? Check your opinion and compare it with that of the author at the bottom of the page.

COUNSELING

True *False*

1. Improves productivity of your business when employees feel listened to and supported.

2. Reduces turnover when employees feel they can vent their thoughts and feelings and deal with problems openly and constructively.

3. Makes your job easier by giving you warning of resistance or problems that may occur following changes.

4. Increases efficiency of your business when you understand the motives and needs of each employee and how he or she will react to organizational events.

5. Reduces conflict and preserves self-esteem when parties are really listened to.

6. Helps you solve problems before they occur.

7. Improves your decision-making when everyone's ideas are heard and employees' strengths and abilities are complemented.

8. Improves your career opportunities when you are known as a manager who can motivate employees and build constructive working relationships with bosses and peers.

9. Increases self-knowledge and personal satisfaction in your job.

10. Improves your self-confidence.

Answers: The author knows that all ten statements are true.
Did you agree?

Coaching and Counseling

THIS IS NEITHER COACHING NOR COUNSELING

THE BENEFITS OF COACHING

Why should you improve your coaching skills? See if you agree with the author by deciding which statements are true and which are false. Compare your answers with those of the author at the bottom of the page.

COACHING

True **False**

☐ ☐ 1. Makes your job easier when employees build their skill levels.

☐ ☐ 2. Enables greater delegation so you can have more time to truly manage versus "do for."

☐ ☐ 3. Builds your reputation as a people developer.

☐ ☐ 4. Increases productivity when employees know what the goals are and how to achieve them.

☐ ☐ 5. Develops sharing of leadership responsibilities.

☐ ☐ 6. Positive recognition and feedback increases employee motivation and initiative.

☐ ☐ 7. Increases likelihood of tasks being completed in a quality way.

☐ ☐ 8. Avoids surprises and defensiveness in performance appraisals.

☐ ☐ 9. Increases creativity and innovation of unit as employees feel safe to take risks.

☐ ☐ 10. Increases team cohesiveness due to clarified goals and roles.

Answers: If you thought all ten statements were true, then you agree with the author.

WHY MANAGERS AVOID COUNSELING

Assume you know the benefits of counseling but still avoid it. If this describes you, take heart—you are not alone. Other managers gave the following reasons why they avoid counseling. Check any reasons that describe why *you* avoid it.

I avoid counseling because:

☐   1. I don't have time.

☐   2. Feelings are personal and not my business.

☐   3. Counseling is for psychologists and psychiatrists.

☐   4. Counseling feels awkward.

☐   5. The employee won't listen to advice.

☐   6. I think feelings about organizational changes are a waste of time and I just want to get the job done.

☐   7. Feelings and concerns may go away.

☐   8. I fear my own feelings.

☐   9. I am afraid to give the wrong advice and be blamed for it.

☐ 10. Employee's career decisions are personal.

☐ 11. I fear uncovering frustration, complaints and dissatisfaction.

☐ 12. I feel responsible for solving the problems of the employee when I have enough problems of my own.

☐ 13. I lack self-confidence and know-how.

☐ 14. Employee may become dependent on me for empathy and advice.

☐ 15. Performance problems will resolve themselves.

☐ 16. I don't know how to explore or manage my own career let alone those of others.

☐ 17. I feel a loss of control when the employee cries or gets angry.

☐ 18. I don't have any solutions for the problems.

☐ 19. I overidentify with the employee's feelings or situations and can't be objective.

☐ 20. I don't have faith in the employee.

WHY MANAGERS AVOID COACHING

Do you find yourself avoiding coaching? Following are 20 typical reasons why managers avoid coaching. Check those that describe why *you* avoid coaching.

I avoid coaching because:

☐   1. I don't have time.

☐   2. Fear of failure.

☐   3. I don't want to scare or overwhelm a new employee.

☐   4. Coaching feels awkward.

☐   5. Nobody coached me; I have no role model.

☐   6. I have too many employees.

☐   7. I didn't set initial goals with employee.

☐   8. Employee won't listen.

☐   9. Employee should be able to figure things out on their own.

☐ 10. Employee will think something is seriously wrong.

☐ 11. Employee doesn't ask for help.

☐ 12. Performance is ''almost'' acceptable.

☐ 13. I will feel threatened.

☐ 14. Employee is motivated and doesn't need feedback.

☐ 15. Employee gets defensive.

☐ 16. Employee needs a certain period of learning time.

☐ 17. I get defensive.

☐ 18. My standards are obvious; employee should know what to do.

☐ 19. Nobody coached me.

☐ 20. I don't care whether the employee is developed.

CHARACTERISTICS OF EFFECTIVE COUNSELORS

Below are 20 characteristics employees have used to describe bosses who are effective counselors. Please rate yourself below:

Scoring Key:

1 Seldom displayed **2** Sometimes displayed **3** Almost Always displayed

As a counselor, I:	Seldom	Sometimes	Almost Always
1. Treat employee's feelings as facts	1	2	3
2. Keep confidences	1	2	3
3. Facilitate discussions	1	2	3
4. Build employee's self-esteem	1	2	3
5. Reassure employee who is insecure	1	2	3
6. Support employee taking risks	1	2	3
7. Solicit employee's feelings, ideas and solutions	1	2	3
8. Let employee make own decisions	1	2	3
9. Care about employee	1	2	3
10. Am empathetic about employee's feelings	1	2	3
11. Help employee work out tough priorities	1	2	3
12. Am patient	1	2	3

	Seldom	Sometimes	Almost Always
13. Give full attention to discussion and am not distracted	1	2	3
14. Make employee feel confident about his/her ability to solve problems	1	2	3
15. Allow employee to vent dissatisfaction or concern with job	1	2	3
16. Consider employee's interests, skills and values when delegating work	1	2	3
17. Consider employee's goals when discussing career opportunities	1	2	3
18. Allow employee to grieve over a loss, personal or professional	1	2	3
19. Avoid acting like the expert on solving personal problems	1	2	3
20. Have sense of humor about organizational life	1	2	3
Total	_____	_____	_____
Grand Total			_____

Scoring:

A total of **50–60** = Excellent; **40–49** = Fair to Good; below 40 = Needs Improvement

Now choose three characteristics that need the most improvement and write them below.

1. _____   2. _____   3. _____

The following page has an assessment for you to photocopy.* Give it to one or more of your employees who is capable of assessing your skills as a counselor.

_____

*Permission to photocopy for personal use only.

EFFECTIVE COUNSELOR ASSESSMENT

_____   _____
Date   Employee's Name

Thank you for taking the time to help me. I am interested in your honest feedback of my skills and attitudes. To be the best manager, I need and want your candid responses.

Scoring Key:

1 Seldom displayed   **2** Sometimes displayed   **3** Almost Always displayed

As my boss, you:	Seldom	Sometimes	Almost Always
1. Treat my feelings as facts	1	2	3
2. Keep confidences	1	2	3
3. Facilitate discussions	1	2	3
4. Build my self-esteem	1	2	3
5. Reassure me when I feel insecure	1	2	3
6. Support me when I take risks	1	2	3
7. Solicit my feelings, ideas and solutions	1	2	3
8. Let me make my own decisions	1	2	3
9. Care about me	1	2	3

	Seldom	Sometimes	Almost Always
10. Are empathetic about my feelings	1	2	3
11. Help me work out tough priorities	1	2	3
12. Are patient	1	2	3
13. Give full attention to discussion	1	2	3
14. Make me feel confident in my ability to solve problems	1	2	3
15. Allow me to vent my dissatisfaction or concern with my job	1	2	3
16. Consider my interests, skills and values when delegating work to me	1	2	3
17. Consider my career goals when discussing career opportunities	1	2	3
18. Allow me to grieve over a loss, personal or professional	1	2	3
19. Avoid acting like the expert on solving personal problems	1	2	3
20. Have a sense of humor about organizational life	1	2	3

CHARACTERISTICS OF EFFECTIVE COACHES

Below are the 20 charactertistics employees have used to describe bosses who are effective coaches. Please rate yourself below:

Scoring Key:

1 Seldom displayed   **2** Sometimes displayed   **3** Almost Always displayed

As a coach, I:	Seldom	Sometimes	Almost Always
1. Capitalize on employee's strengths	1	2	3
2. Give employees visibility	1	2	3
3. Provide freedom to do job	1	2	3
4. Set standards of excellence	1	2	3
5. Orient employee to company values and business strategy	1	2	3
6. Hold employee accountable	1	2	3
7. Protect employee from undue stress	1	2	3
8. Encourage employee when he/she is discouraged or about to undertake new or difficult assignments	1	2	3
9. Provide information about the company and the employee's role in the attainment of company goals	1	2	3
10. Make performance expectations and priorities clear	1	2	3
11. Take time to build trust	1	2	3
12. Provide appropriate training and support when needed	1	2	3

	Seldom	Sometimes	Almost Always
13. Solicit and listen to ideas	1	2	3
14. View employees as partners and critical to the success of the unit	1	2	3
15. Serve as a good role model	1	2	3
16. Won't let employee give up	1	2	3
17. Don't divulge confidences	1	2	3
18. Explain reasons for decisions and procedures and give advance notice of changes whenever possible	1	2	3
19. Provide employees with regular feedback about their job performance	1	2	3
20. Give employees credit when they deserve it	1	2	3
Total	___	___	___
Grand Total	___	___	___

Scoring:

A total of **50–60** = Excellent; **40–49** = Fair to Good; below 40 = Needs Improvement

Now choose three characteristics that need the most improvement and write them below.

1. _____   2. _____   3. _____

The following page has an assessment for you to photocopy.* Give it to one or more of your employees who is capable of assessing your skills as a coach.

---

*Permission to photocopy for personal use only.

EFFECTIVE COACH ASSESSMENT

_____   _____
Date   Employee's Name

Thank you for taking the time to help me. I am interested in your honest feedback of my skills and attitudes as a coach. Please be honest. To be the best manager, I need and want your candid responses.

Scoring Key:

1 Seldom displayed   **2** Sometimes displayed   **3** Almost Always displayed

As my boss, you:	Seldom	Sometimes	Almost Always
1. Capitalize on my strengths	1	2	3
2. Give me visibility	1	2	3
3. Provide freedom to do my job	1	2	3
4. Set standards of excellence	1	2	3
5. Orient me to company values and business strategy	1	2	3
6. Hold me accountable	1	2	3
7. Protect me from undue stress	1	2	3
8. Encourage me when I'm discouraged or about to undertake a new or difficult assignment	1	2	3
9. Provide information about the company and my role in the attainment of company goals	1	2	3

	Seldom	Sometimes	Almost Always
10. Make performance expectations and priorities clear	1	2	3
11. Take time to build trust	1	2	3
12. Provide appropriate training and support when needed	1	2	3
13. Solicit and listens to my ideas	1	2	3
14. View me as a partner who is critical to the success of the unit	1	2	3
15. Serve as a good role model	1	2	3
16. Won't let me give up	1	2	3
17. Don't divulge confidences	1	2	3
18. Explain reasons for decisions and procedures and give advance notice of changes whenever possible	1	2	3
19. Provide me with regular feedback about my job performance	1	2	3
20. Give me credit when I deserve it	1	2	3
Total	____	____	____

Coaching and Counseling

REVIEW

You have now completed Section I. Can you recognize the differences between coaching and counseling? Do you have an understanding of when to use them?

If the answer is no, review the appropriate parts of Section I.

If the answer is yes, you are ready for Section II: When Should You Counsel or Coach?

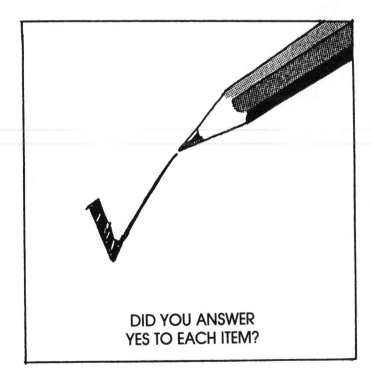

DID YOU ANSWER
YES TO EACH ITEM?

SECTION

II

When Should You Counsel or Coach?

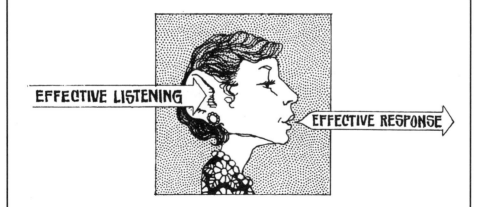

EFFECTIVE LISTENING

EFFECTIVE RESPONSE

WHEN TO COUNSEL OR COACH?

Knowing when to counsel or coach is an important skill. It is the first step in the coaching or counseling process. When you can identify, in a timely manner, situations that need your expertise you are on your way to becoming an effective manager.

As you read through the following work situations, remember that they may not only apply to an employee reporting to you but to a peer, a boss or even to yourself.

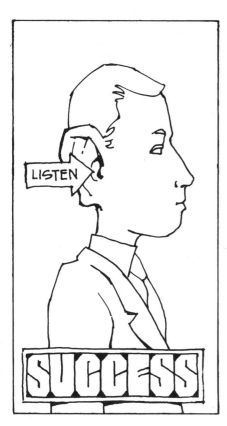

A SUCCESSFUL COACH OR COUNSELOR LISTENS MORE THAN TALKS

WORK SITUATIONS THAT MAY REQUIRE COUNSELING

Check any that you have personally encountered:

☐ 1. Reorganizations

☐ 2. Layoffs—counseling for those who are laid off *and* those who are not

☐ 3. Demotions due to organization changes

☐ 4. Salary freezes; decreases in salary, status or responsibility

☐ 5. Employee faced with other career opportunities inside or outside of the organization

☐ 6. Employee faced with no career opportunities inside the organizaton

☐ 7. Employee unhappy with you as boss

☐ 8. Employee unhappy with work assignment

☐ 9. Employee who has conflict with peer

☐ 10. Employee that feels stressed, burned out, or is having a grief reaction due to loss.

☐ 11. Employee who feels insecure about skills or ability to do the job

☐ 12. Employee quitting to take new job

☐ 13. Employee who has been promoted and is scared

☐ 14. Employee that shares personal problem requiring support

☐ 15. Employee whose personal problems are affecting performance of others

☐ 16. Performance problems that persist

☐ 17. Employee who is experiencing failure

☐ 18. Employee who is dissappointed in new job

Can you think of any other situations from your personal experience where counseling would have been effective?

19. _____

20. _____

WORK SITUATIONS THAT MAY REQUIRE COACHING

Check any that you have personally encountered:

☐   1.   Orientation and training of a new employee

☐   2.   Teaching a new job skill

☐   3.   Need to explain standards of the work unit

☐   4.   Need to explain cultural norms and political realities of the organization

☐   5.   Simple corrections to performance are required

☐   6.   Goals or business conditions change

☐   7.   You are new to a group

☐   8.   Employees facing new work experience

☐   9.   Employee that needs help setting priorities

☐   10.   Follow up to a training session

☐   11.   Employee that displays low or moderate performance

☐   12.   Employee who needs reinforcement for good performance

☐   13.   Employee wants to become a peak performer

☐   14.   Formal or informal performance reviews

☐   15.   Employee needs preparation to meet his/her future career goals

☐   16.   Employee needs preparation for more challenging work assignment

☐   17.   Employee needs self-confidence developed

☐   18.   When power or control battles are affecting team cohesiveness

---

Can you think of any other situations that may require coaching?

19. _____

20. _____

SYMPTOMS OF PERFORMANCE PROBLEMS

If an employee comes to you with a specific problem, great—your job as a manager has just been made easier. But how about those employees who never walk through your door even though you say your "door is always open." You may have to rely on your observation and analytical skills to recognize signs of performance problems, and then try to determine the root cause.

SIGNS OF DECLINING PERFORMANCE

1. Decreased productivity
2. Poor quality work
3. Missed due dates
4. Doing small task first
5. Avoiding tougher jobs
6. Disorganized
7. Leaning on others for direction
8. Away from desk for long periods
9. Upward delegation
10. Absenteeism

Add others:

_____

_____

_____

_____

11. Little or no initiative
12. Withdrawn
13. Disinterested
14. Increased complaining
15. Uncooperative
16. Blaming failure on others
17. Defensive
18. Avoids contact with others on team
19. Lacking enthusiasm for job
20. Irritability, depression

Add others:

_____

_____

_____

_____

In the next section we will begin to explore some possible root causes of these symptoms.

WHY EMPLOYEES DON'T GET
THE JOB DONE—ROOT CAUSES

There are generally three root causes of performance problems:

SKILL DEFICITS
MOTIVATIONAL DEFICITS
RESOURCE DEFICITS

SKILL DEFICITS

They Don't Know How to Do the Job

ASK YOURSELF THESE FIVE QUESTIONS TO DETERMINE IF THERE IS A SKILL DEFICIT:

▶ Did you analyze the skills required for this job and match it to the employee's background BEFORE you hired them? Did you get evidence that they had the right set of skills?

▶ Did you orient or coach the employee about the workplace and culture and explain how you want things done *here?*

▶ Did you set performance expectations and standards with the employee so they knew what to do? Does the employee know what is expected?

▶ Did you talk to the employee to be sure your communication was clear and complete? Did you include the employee in the goal setting process?

▶ Have you trained the employee in the skills required to do the job? Is there time for you to do it? If not, who else on the team can coach or train this employee?

MOTIVATIONAL DEFICITS

They Don't Want to Do the Job—Now or Forever?

ASK YOURSELF THESE FIVE QUESTIONS TO DETERMINE IF THERE IS A MOTIVATIONAL DEFICIT:

► Do they really want this job?

► Does the job utilize their skills, values and interests? Is the job monotonous and unstimulating? Can you redesign the job to make it more interesting?

► Do you hold the employee accountable for meeting the goals and standards?

► Do you provide regular effective feedback to sustain or improve performance?

► Is there a sudden drop in performance that was once moderate to high? Has the employee demonstrated the skills in the job before? Is this drop situational (due to a personal problem or change in the employees personal life) or a chronic problem that has a pattern of sporadic performance drops? Is it temporary or permanent?

Sometimes motivational deficits can be caused by personal problems that are long term and chronic or short term and temporary. The manager must assess the performance history to determine if it is a reactive or long term problem. While a manager's job is to focus on performance, it is crucial that managers can detect personal problems that can undermine performance and know what type of interventions and resources to utilize in order to save a normally productive employee.

In the next section we explore some common human problems that can affect productivity.

Consider the use of an employee assistance professional if the scope of the problem is beyond you, your role and your training.

RESOURCE DEFICITS

Can Anyone Really Do This Job?
Is the Employee Getting Burned-Out?

ASK YOURSELF THESE FIVE QUESTIONS TO DETERMINE IF THERE IS A RESOURCE DEFICIT:

► Does the pace and homogeneity of the work make employees bone weary? Can you change the pace or create more diversity in the tasks?

► Is the work highly interpersonal in nature with a lot of conflict or confrontation with no break? Can you build in solitary time for the employee to regroup? Is the work highly technical and complex in nature? Does it require solitude and quiet concentration? Does the workplace provide this? Can you create it?

► Is the employee managing time resources and priorities effectively? If not, can you send him or her to a relevant time management course or coach them in techniques?

► Is there just too much work coming their way too fast? How can you streamline the systems that support the work in getting done? Modify reports, meetings, procedures to save the employee time and energy?

► What additional resources or training can you give the employee to handle the volume so you can keep the employee functional and satisfied?

PERSONAL PROBLEMS THAT MAY AFFECT JOB PERFORMANCE

In this section, we will explore four frequent personal problems that occur in the work place. A manager may have to be skilled in detecting these in order to keep a valuable employee or defuse a potentially violent situation. The idea is not to turn the manager into a psychiatrist, but to provide some general guidelines for assessing the root cause of performance problems and suggestions of recommended actions to take.

DEPRESSION

While it is not a manager's job to diagnose clinical depression, it is their job to observe, analyze, and document behaviors related to job performance and make sure that employees know there are professional resources available to assist them with transitions, losses or problems in their personal lives that could affect job performance.

Mental illness is covered by the Americans with Disabilities Act (ADA) of 1990, which mandates that employers make a reasonable accommodation for disabled employees. This could mean being flexible about schedules so an employee can adjust to a medication and benefit from psychotherapy with a professional.

When analyzing the root cause of performance problems major clinical depression should be distinguished from normal temporary grief reactions due to losses in one's personal or professional life. Major clinical depressions can last for months or years.

To assist you in analyzing the root cause of performance problems, review the following warning signs if you suspect one of your employees may be depressed.

ASSESSING WARNING SIGNS OF DEPRESSION

1. Loss of interest in the work and of the people on the job
2. Difficulty concentrating, remembering things or making decisions
3. Irritability or tearfulness
4. Absenteeism
5. Frequent comments about being tired all the time
6. Frequent complaints about physical problems, aches and pains
7. A change in eating habits—a recent weight gain or loss of more than ten pounds
8. Decreased productivity and difficulty in meeting deadlines
9. Negative comments about themselves, their abilities, accomplishments, speed in learning new things
10. Napping on the job

WHAT TO DO NEXT: TEN TIPS

☐ Document the changes in job performance in terms of specific behaviors.

☐ Research your companies written policies about disciplinary discussions.

☐ Use the counseling techniques recommended in this book to conduct a discussion focusing on job performance with the employee.

☐ Use active listening techniques to draw the employee out and determine if this is a reaction to a loss or a chronic condition affecting job performance.

☐ Suggest to the employee that they may need help getting back on course and refer the employee to an employee assistance program or professional.

☐ Tell them it is their choice whether to seek help but that you will expect job performance to improve.

☐ Let them know that what happens at the Employee Assistance Program is confidential.

☐ Do not diagnose or even suggest they may have an illness.

☐ If they decide to seek treatment, adjust work schedules and work load if possible for a defined period so the employee gets up to speed.

☐ Let the employee know that you consider them a valuable employee.

GRIEF REACTIONS

There have been major transformations in the workplace and these changes can directly affect people, their work and personal lives. Workers can no longer assume any long term job stability. They have to learn to manage their own careers and may have to meet greater performance demands.

Change can often mean loss of security, friends, control, long time dreams, or even self-esteem. Loss can often feel as if a form of death has occurred and can trigger grief reactions. We, as humans, mourn for the loss of loved ones, as well as hopes, unrealized goals, and even status. It is important for managers to realize that it is *normal* to grieve when a loss occurs. Grief is a set of behaviors that come from loss or the threat of loss. While most people will feel some anger, sadness or anxiety, grief reactions vary from person to person, in terms of severity and longevity. This is dependent on their coping skills, previous losses, how they perceive the current loss, and how much support they get during the transition period.

ASSESSING WARNING SIGNS OF GRIEF REACTIONS*

1. Anger, irritability

2. Distrust or suspicion

3. Self-doubt

4. Apathy about the work getting done

5. Anxiety about the future

6. Bitter resentment towards management

7. Isolation from others

8. Formal complaints or grievances

9. Lack of willingness to take risks or try new things

10. Territorial behaviors— clinging to resources, titles, etc.

---

*For a more comprehensive view on this subject, read the Crisp book *Coping with Workplace Change: Dealing with Loss and Grief* by J. Shep Jeffreys, Ed.D.

WHAT TO DO NEXT: TEN TIPS

☐ Encourage employees to talk about their feelings by using active listening. Validate their feelings.

☐ Provide information about the changes that are happening and help employees explore what it means to them.

☐ Help them let go by having some rituals to say goodbye to the past.

☐ Acknowledge the contributions of people in the past.

☐ Build in some "lag time" in your productivity schedules to allow people to grieve.

☐ Talk about the vision and goals for the future—yours and theirs.

☐ Communicate what new skills or knowledge will be needed in the future.

☐ Help employees make the necessary changes for their new work situation.

☐ Do some team building activities to encourage people to bond and support each other.

☐ Take care of your own feelings and work them through so you don't project your upsets onto your employees.

HOSTILITY (THAT COULD LEAD TO VIOLENCE)

Hostility can lead to various levels of disruption in the workplace. It can begin as simple insubordination, conflict with peers, and threats and escalate to murder, suicide or even arson. Experts use the term *critical incident* to describe events that could potentially lead to workplace violence. Critical incidents can include refusal to follow company policy, antagonism toward customers, verbal wishes to hurt coworkers and/or management, and actual threats of a sexual or violent nature. Though often ignored or minimized by coworkers and management, it is crucial that these critical incidents are seen as warning signs and dealt with immediately, with positive management strategies.

For the purpose of this book, workplace violence is defined as any situation that may increase in intensity and threaten the safety of any employee; have an impact on any employee's physical and/or psychological well-being and/or cause damage to company property.

Although accurate predictions of violence are difficult to make, the best indicator of future behavior is past behavior. Indeed, the best predictor of future violence is a history of violence.

Violent people often give out many clues—even progressively serious clues—that they might violently act out their frustration. The tragedy of workplace violence occurs when these clues are not recognized, or are not revealed to the next level of management. In this section you will find some tools to help you identify and evaluate indications of possible violent tendencies.

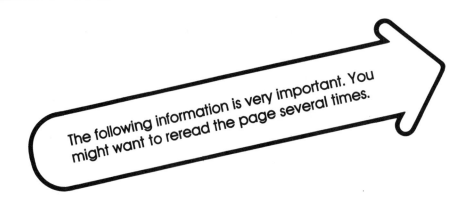

The following information is very important. You might want to reread the page several times.

ASSESSING WARNING SIGNS OF HOSTILITY
(THAT COULD LEAD TO VIOLENCE)

1. Intimidation of others

2. Angry outbursts; low tolerance for frustration, holds grudges

3. Sullen withdrawal or suspicious of others' motives

4. Substance abuse

5. Lacks control of impulses

6. Financial or family problems, or is socially isolated

7. Blames others for mistakes and difficulties, is defensive when criticized

8. Ominous threats, or conflict with boss or coworker

9. Obsessions/stalking/history of family violence

10. Owns or discusses weapons

WHAT TO DO AFTER A CRITICAL INCIDENT: TEN TIPS*

☐ Recognize signs of trouble and take action early

☐ Take all threats seriously

☐ Assemble a crisis management team to review procedures

☐ Create a crisis management plan

☐ Mobilize professional advisors to analyze behavior, threats and potential for future violence

☐ Investigate and interview people about the incident

☐ Meet with hostile employee and listen to his or her point of view

☐ Provide coaching or counseling

☐ Take appropriate disciplinary action if the performance problem is long-standing and there is evidence of abusive behavior

☐ Provide protection for those threatened

---

*For a comprehensive view on this subject, read Crisp Publications' *Preventing Workplace Violence* by Marianne Minor.

CHEMICAL DEPENDENCY

Chemical dependency is a fairly common workplace problem, as approximately one out of six workers abuse alcohol or drugs. It is important that managers learn as much as they can about this problem and how it affects work performance. Managers must learn to recognize the warning signs, to conduct effective coaching and counseling discussions with employees about job performance, but should leave the diagnosis and treatment to substance abuse experts.

Chemical dependency is a disease characterized by loss of control. When abuse creates negative impacts on major life areas, and the person continues to use the substance, it can be considered an addiction. Abuse and addiction usually create negative impact in all life areas such as health, family and marital problems, financial difficulties, poor relationships with friends, and legal problems, such as arrest for drunk driving. In the workplace there is a deterioration in work performance quality, quantity or both.

Review the warning signs below to determine a possible root cause of a performance problem.

ASSESSING WARNING SIGNS OF CHEMICAL DEPENDENCY

1. A decline in work quality or quantity
2. Emotional peaks and valleys—increase in mood swings
3. Conflicts, resentments, or hostile interactions with coworkers
4. Missed deadlines
5. Complaints from customers, or other colleagues about sloppy work or angry outbursts
6. Accidents that could cause injury to self or others
7. Unexplained absences from the workplace—long lunches, excessive breaks
8. Defensiveness or irrational excuses when confronted with not meeting job expectations
9. An increase in health problems causing attendance problems
10. Lacking of attention to detail and/or lack of concentration

WHAT TO DO NEXT: TEN TIPS

☐ Do not enable the employee by preventing them from experiencing the consequences of his or her behavior—do not make excuses for their behavior or accept poor performance.

☐ Clearly identify the signs of declining performance early and take constructive action.

☐ Know your company policy around substance abuse problems.

☐ Make sure performance expectations are clear.

☐ Document discussions around performance and action plans that are agreed upon.

☐ Monitor performance after an action plan has been established and recognize performance improvements.

☐ Follow the guidelines in this book on coaching and counseling to avoid making the employee hostile or defensive during your discussions.

☐ Know the professional resources available to help you develop a plan and for the employee to obtain professional treatment.

☐ Be prepared with the list of appropriate referrals if the employee admits there is a problem or you suggest there may be a problem with their job performance.

☐ Let employees know you consider them valuable.

---

*For a more comprehensive view on the subject, read the Crisp book *Job Performance and Chemical Dependency* by Robert Maddux and Lynda Voorhees.

CASE STUDIES TO EVALUATE YOUR SKILLS

Each of the five cases below describe typical situations a manager or supervisor can encounter on the job. Please specify what you feel is required: counseling, coaching, or both. Compare your answers with those of the author on the following page.

1. You have just hired Miguel who has a degree in Engineering. He has lots of energy and enthusiasm for his new job and is a project leader. You want to get him off on the right start.

   Counsel ☐ **Coach** ☐

2. Sally has been with your unit for one year now. She has just been promoted to Marketing Manager. She has shown creativity in her marketing campaigns and lots of drive. She has extremely high standards of performance, and pushes herself and others equally hard. Unfortunately, her behavior seems to have created a morale problem in her unit. She has her unit working overtime and weekends as she attempts to oversee every detail. Sally demands perfection. You have had several complaints from her employees.

   Counsel ☐ **Coach** ☐

3. Susan, Supervisor of Facilities, has been working for you for three years. She has been a superstar, increasing productivity in her unit by more than 70 percent in the last year. Due to her tremendous talents in managing people you have offered her a promotion to Manager of Facilities. She has stopped by your office to talk about her fears and insecurities regarding the new position. You have no doubt that she can do it well.

   Counsel ☐ **Coach** ☐

4. Wei-Ling is a production operator who has been a conscientious employee with a good track record. She shows a lot of initiative and enthusiasm for her job. She has stopped by your office to discuss a personal problem that may interfere with her job—she has just discovered that her mother is dying of cancer. She is close to her mother and seems very upset.

   Counsel ☐ **Coach** ☐

5. Joe, one of your QC inspectors, has been with your group for six months. His performance has been substandard in many ways. He shows up late for work at least two days a week, is disruptive in departmental meetings and has let many defective parts pass through his station.

   Counsel ☐ **Coach** ☐

ANSWERS TO CASE STUDIES

1. **COACH** Miguel is a newcomer and needs direction, orientation and probably training.

2. **COACH** Sally needs direction and training on how to be a manager, i.e. setting realistic goals and using recognition to motivate employees. If after your coaching she continues to drive her unit hard, you may need to *counsel* her.

3. **COUNSEL** Susan is seeking you out to discuss her feelings. Her skills are not deficient.

4. **COUNSEL** Wei-Ling has initiated discussion about a personal problem that may affect her work.

5. **COACH** Joe needs to understand the job standards and the importance of being on time, as well as the consequences of his performance. If his problems persist after your coaching session, he may require counseling.

How did you do? If your answers agreed with those of the author, then you are ready to go on to Section III. If you didn't agree with the answers, review the appropriate parts of Section II.

SECTION

III

Giving and Receiving Feedback

HOW YOU CAN GIVE AND RECEIVE EFFECTIVE FEEDBACK

You should now know what coaching and counseling involve and when you should use each. Now you are ready to learn the most important skill to becoming an effective coach or counselor—namely how to provide effective feedback that helps employees improve performance.

Whether you recognize it or not, you are constantly providing feedback. How you provide that feedback will often spell the difference between success or failure.

FOUR TYPES OF FEEDBACK

TYPE 1	DEFINITION	PURPOSE	IMPACT
SILENCE	No response provided. No news is *not* good news!	Maintain status quo	• Decreases confidence (long term) • Reduces performance (long term) • Creates surprises during performance appraisals • Can create paranoia and insecurity

TYPE 2	DEFINITION	PURPOSE	IMPACT
CRITICISM (negative)	Identifies behaviors or results that *were* undesirable, not up to standard. Example: "Sue, you did a poor job running that meeting this morning."	Stop undesirable behavior/results	• Generates excuses and blaming of others • Tends to eliminate other related behaviors • Decreases confidence and self esteem • Leads to escape and avoidance of manager and work • Hurts relationship

TYPE 3	DEFINITION	PURPOSE	IMPACT
ADVICE	Identifies behaviors or results that are highly regarded and often specifies how to incorporate them in the future. Example: ''Sue, Let's discuss some guidelines on conducting effective meetings before your next staff meeting so you feel good about the process.''	Shape or change behavior/results to increase performance	• Improves confidence • Can improve relationship • Increase performance

TYPE 4	DEFINITION	PURPOSE	IMPACT
REINFORCEMENT (positive)	Identifies behavior or results that *were* desired; up to or exceeding standards. Example: ''Sue, I noticed how you planned and posted an agenda before your meeting today. I think it really kept the meeting focused.''	Increase desired performance/results	• Increases confidence • Increases performance • Increases motivation • Increases willingness to take on new tasks and be more visible.

HOW DO YOU USE FEEDBACK?

Think about the type of feedback you use in managing your employees. Then take the following quiz.

When I manage, I use this type of feedback:	Almost Always	Frequently	Occasionally	Never
1. Silence	☐	☐	☐	☐
2. Criticism (Negative)	☐	☐	☐	☐
3. Reinforcement (Positive)	☐	☐	☐	☐
4. Advice	☐	☐	☐	☐

WHAT KIND OF FEEDBACK DO YOU USE?

FEEDBACK MEMORIES: PAINFUL AND PLEASANT

Many times throughout our lives we receive feedback. Sometimes it is given directly, sometimes indirectly. Sometimes the feedback is positive, sometimes negative. If we are fortunate, the feedback helps us learn something about ourselves. But sometimes feedback creates negative feelings and does little to improve our performance.

Think about an "unforgettable negative feedback experience" where the feedback given created negative feelings in you and answer the following statements:

1. Describe what it was about the way the feedback was given that created such a negative effect.

2. Was the feedback solicited or imposed?

3. What impact did this feedback have on your feelings and subsequent performance?

Now try to remember a time when you received positive feedback that increased your self-esteem and motivation and respond in the space provided:

1. Describe what it was about the way the feedback was given that created such a positive effect.

2. Was the feedback solicited or imposed?

3. What impact did this feedback have on your feelings and subsequent performance?

HOW TO GIVE EFFECTIVE FEEDBACK

1. **Make your feedback specific as related to behavior.**

   Good: "Henry, I am concerned about your punctuality. You have been 15 minutes late for the last three mornings, please explain why."

   Bad: "Henry, you have a lousy attitude towards your job."

2. **Consider your timing, either before the event in the form of advice, or immediately after it as positive feedback.**

   Good: (advice before) "Sally, I'd like to review the content of your presentation with you before your speech next week so you can really do a "good" job in front of the group."

   Bad: (criticism after) "Sally, because you've done such a poor job in the past, I need to preview the speech you plan on giving next week."

   Good: (positive after) "Sally, you did an outstanding job in organizing your presentation for the meeting. The speech was well-researched and logical."

3. **Consider the needs of the person receiving the feedback as well as your own. Ask yourself what he or she will get out of the information. Are you "dumping" or genuinely attempting to improve performance or the relationship?**

   Good: "Sue, I know how important it is to you to get the newsletter just right, and recognize you're under a lot of pressure right now. I will help you edit it this time, but I want you to take that editing class so you can handle it solo in the future."

   Bad: "Sue, you always need help with the newsletter. It's not my responsibility. Don't you think it's about time you learned how to edit the newsletter?"

4. **Focus on behavior the receiver can do something about.**

   Good: "Sam, we would appreciate you keeping the team informed about the status of the project? How about scheduling a weekly status meeting?"

   Bad: "Sam, why are you are so shy that you don't like to talk to other people?"

5. **Solicit feedback rather than impose it.**

   Good: "Linda, I heard you say you would like to learn how to handle your most difficult customer more effectively? Would you like me to share some techniques I have seen work?"

   Bad: "Linda, I saw the way you handled Mrs. Dawson during this crisis. It really stinks."

6. **Avoid labels and judgements by describing rather than evaluating behavior.**

   Good: "Steve, I have given you five chances to attend training programs in the last year and you haven't enrolled yet. What's getting in your way?"

   Bad: "Steve, you are very lazy about improving your skills and don't seem to care about your career here."

7. **Define the impact on you, the unit, the team and the company.**

   Good: "Sarah, when you don't get your report to me on time, I can't get my report to my boss on time. This slows up decisions about resources needed for next month."

   Bad: "Sarah, can't you ever get your reports to me on time?"

8. **Use "I" statements as opposed to "you" statements to reduce defensiveness and ask for a change in behavior.**

   Good: "Tim, when you play your radio in the work area I lose my concentration. Would you mind turning it off during regular work hours?"

   Bad: "Tim, you are so inconsiderate of other people when you leave your radio on."

9. **Check to be sure clear communication has occurred.**

   Good: "Mary, do you know the procedure for recording all my phone messages? Can you you go over the procedure to be sure I covered everything?"

   Bad: "Mary, I'm sure you got it all, huh?"

10. **Give the feedback in a calm, unemotional language, tone and body language.**

    Good: "Joe, I'm sure your progress will be much faster now that you are clear on how to use this new machinery."

    Bad: "Joe, isn't it about time you improved your production with this machine!"

ADDITIONAL POINTS TO REMEMBER

1. Reinforcement is the most effective form of feedback. Discipline yourself to catch employees doing things right and using their strengths.

2. Criticism is the most ineffective form of feedback. It can damage self-esteem.

3. The difference between criticism and advice is a difference in *timing*. Most criticism can be reframed as advice.

4. When feedback is mixed the impact is diluted. The employee ends up confused and not knowing what to do. They may not leave the discussion with a clear understanding of what to do differently.

5. Criticism overpowers all other feedback. Feedback should build relationships, not destroy them.

6. Silence is not always "golden." It can be interpreted in a variety of ways.

POSITIVE FEEDBACK COMES IN MANY FORMS

Let employees know what specifically you appreciate about them, their work, their involvement, their attitude. Use the list below to brainstorm your own unique reinforcers.

25 Kinds of Reinforcement

1. Allow your employees to develop their own work styles as long as the work gets done satisfactorily.
2. Let each person know when their work or some part of it has improved.
3. Give employees books related to their interests and career goals.
4. Show an interest in their personal lives—ask about their kids, spouses, vacations.
5. In a family crisis, give time off with pay.
6. Have ice cream socials to celebrate team milestones.
7. Take the team to lunch to introduce a new member of the team.
8. Create a pleasant workplace—provide good chairs, adequate lighting, temperature controls, clean restrooms with walls freshly painted.
9. Provide employees with lap top computers so they can work anywhere and keep in touch.
10. Provide good food and coffee during long meetings or conferences.
11. Have dress down days at the end of difficult projects.
12. Send flowers to their homes on special occasions.
13. Honor them at all employee meetings by talking about their contributions.
14. Fit the job to the personalities and skills of employees rather than the other way around.
15. Take the employees and their spouses to a restaurant to celebrate milestones.
16. In a family crisis, give time off with pay.
17. Have a Christmas party, or, if funds are tight, give everyone a turkey.
18. Have farewell and retirement parties and talk about the value the employee gave to the company.
19. Let employees leave early or take long lunches if business is slow or after a grueling project is finished.
20. Remind yourself that people need balance in their lives and don't expect them to work around the clock week after week.
21. Have brown bag lunches with speakers for employees on their areas of interest.
22. When a project has a tight deadline, pitch in yourself or be available for questions and support.
23. Have quarterly Sensing sessions to solicit feedback and learn how employees feel so you can improve attitude, climate and morale.
24. Give employees bonuses when they exceed their yearly goals.
25. On business trips, make sure employees have a separate and equal room and fly at the same level as you. Take a half day off and visit the local museum together.

WHAT BEHAVIOR DO I REWARD, IGNORE OR PUNISH?

It is crucial for managers to examine how they communicate what is desired or undesired performance and behavior. Take a few moments to write down the behaviors you reward in your unit, behaviors you ignore and behaviors you punish. Think in terms of who gets the best assignments, opportunities, public praise, exposure and benefits.

Behaviors I reward	Behaviors I ignore	Behaviors I punish
_____	_____	_____
_____	_____	_____

How should this be changed?

_____	_____	_____
_____	_____	_____

CASE STUDIES ON GIVING FEEDBACK

WHAT TYPE OF FEEDBACK SHOULD THE MANAGER USE?

Write in the spaces provided the type of feedback you would use and what you would say in each of the following situations. Compare your answers with those of the author on the following page.

A = Advice   **P** = Positive Feedback   **N** = Negative (criticism)   **S** = Silence

1. Fred, a recently hired marketing specialist, has just turned in his first monthly marketing report. Your impression is that the report was done in a hurry and was not well thought out. You did not train Fred in how to develop the report.

You would use _____

What would you say to Fred?

_____

_____

_____

2. Carla has been in charge of materials distribution for the last 12 months. Recently you have received complaints from the production line supervisor that materials have been arriving late at the line.

You would use _____

What would you say to Carla?

_____

_____

_____

3. Paula is your new secretary. She has just given you some letters you asked her to type. They were neat and error-free, and finished on time.

You would use _____

What would you say to Paula?

_____

_____

_____

4. Don has just submitted his part of a proposal you are responsible for coordinating. It is Monday and you know he worked most of the weekend to get his piece to you. His deadline was pretty tight and you are grateful he put in the extra time to meet it. Unfortunately, you are racing-out the door to catch a plane with the proposal in your hand.

You would use _____

What would you say to Don?

_____

_____

_____

ANSWERS TO CASES ON PAGE 51.

1. **ADVICE:** "Fred, let's discuss how I would like to have your reports formatted as well as the content I need in the report. I want you to know who gets the reports and how they are used so you will know why they need to be done in this specific way. You are new and I want you to get off to a good start with these reports."

2. **ADVICE:** "Carla, I'd like to discuss a concern I have with your materials arrival times. Let's discuss what happens when the materials are not on time and the effect it has on other people and departments. Can you let me know what interferes with you getting the materials on time? What can you do about it?"

3. **POSITIVE FEEDBACK:** "Paula, I sure appreciate how well done these letters are! They are neat, have no errors, and were returned to me on time. Thank you."

4. **POSITIVE FEEDBACK:** Send Don a card from the airport or hotel as soon as possible letting him know how much you appreciated him working hard like that and helping you out.

ACTION PLAN FOR GIVING FEEDBACK

Now that you know how important it is to give high-quality feedback, examine the feedback needs of your employees. Analyze who needs what kind of feedback and set a date for a feedback discussion.

Employee	Feedback needs	Date to discuss feedback
1. _____	_____	_____
	_____	
	_____	
2. _____	_____	_____
	_____	
	_____	
3. _____	_____	_____
	_____	
	_____	
4. _____	_____	_____
	_____	
	_____	
5. _____	_____	_____
	_____	
	_____	

BE A ROLE MODEL

Now that you know how important feedback can be to your employees, think about yourself.

How do you receive unsolicited feedback?

_____

_____

_____

Do you solicit feedback from your employees, peers or boss on how you can help them?

_____

_____

_____

Remember, you are a role model* and a manager's ability to receive and solicit feedback can be just as important to his or her success as giving it.

Use the following pointers to become a good feedback role model.

5 POINTERS FOR GETTING EFFECTIVE FEEDBACK

1. Use active listening techniques
2. Do not get defensive or justify what happened
3. Try hard to understand the other person's perspective
4. Ask open-ended questions about the other person's views
5. Say thank you

---

*For more information on this topic, read *Coaching for Development* by Marianne Minor, Crisp Publications.

SECTION

IV

Plan and Conduct Counseling and Coaching Sessions

PREPARING FOR A COUNSELING OR COACHING SESSION

When a counseling or coaching session goes poorly, it is usually because the manager has not prepared properly. At this point you should have answered the checklists included in Section II and know which type of session you need to conduct. You have already analyzed whether you are dealing with a skill, motivation or resource deficit.

Now you are ready to prepare for the session on the following page by doing each of the nine items that follow. Put a check mark next to each completed item.

PREPARING FOR A COUNSELING OR COACHING SESSION (continued)

For my next counseling/coaching session I will prepare by completing each of the following steps. Place a ☑.

- ☐ 1. Consider how many sessions I will need, the degree of trust, and the employee's confidence level.

- ☐ 2. Be clear about my reason for the session and define my goals.

- ☐ 3. Review the work goals and past performance of the employee.

- ☐ 4. Give the employee notice of the time and place.

- ☐ 5. Allot a minimum of 30 minutes for the session.

- ☐ 6. Remove all distractions (phone, visitors, etc.) from the meeting place.

- ☐ 7. Remove physical barriers between myself and the employee (e.g., don't sit behind a desk).

- ☐ 8. Write out what I plan to say and rehearse it. Keep my notes in front of me during the session to avoid the feeling of losing control.

- ☐ 9. Plan to take notes to document the session, and develop a record of the corrective action plans and performance improvements.

Want to avoid the pitfalls of counseling and coaching? Read on...

COUNSELING PITFALLS TO AVOID

Following are some pitfalls if managers do not prepare properly. Check those pitfalls that you have experienced or observed.

☐   1. Manager has preconceived notions about what the real problem is.

☐   2. Manager has opinions about employee's choices and judges employee's decisions according to the manager's own values.

☐   3. Manager tells employee what he/she should or ought to do.

☐   4. Manager plays psychiatrist and attempts to diagnose or "treat" employee.

☐   5. Manager downplays employee's problem or pain by using clichés such as "change is wonderful."

☐   6. Manager moves into problem-solving mode from start, rather than listening to employees' feelings.

☐   7. Manager does not empathize with employee's problems or feelings.

☐   8. Manager shifts focus to his/her problems or feelings.

☐   9. Manager over-empathizes with employee's problem or feelings, losing objectivity.

☐ 10. Manager "rescues" employee by taking responsibility for decision making away from the employee.

☐ 11. Manager does not check with Human Resources or Personnel for assistance in problem beyond the manager's scope.

☐ 12. Manager has not investigated company resources such as employee assistance programs to assist in determining the real problem.

Write below any additional pitfalls you need to watch for that are not listed above.

_____

_____

_____

_____

COACHING PITFALLS TO AVOID

Read the following pitfalls managers can fall into if they do not prepare properly. Check those pitfalls that you have experienced.

☐   1. Manager can't determine real problem because they did not analyze performance trends.

☐   2. Manager is unclear about what he/she expects in the way of changes.

☐   3. Manager doesn't have enough information and data to back up their view.

☐   4. Manager exhibits personal bias towards employee or problem.

☐   5. Manager is inflexible about possible solutions.

☐   6. Manager loses control due to employee's hostile reaction.

☐   7. Manager becomes defensive and hostile when questioned for specific examples.

☐   8. Manager doesn't solicit employee's suggestions or solutions.

☐   9. Manager doesn't listen to employee's view of the problem.

☐ 10. Manager fails to document evolving performance problems.

☐ 11. Manager fails to hold employee accountable in follow-up meeting.

☐ 12. Manager fails to reinforce improved performance.

Write below any additional pitfalls you need to watch for that are not listed above.

_____

_____

_____

_____

_____

GUIDELINES FOR CONDUCTING A SUCCESSFUL COUNSELING SESSION

You are ready to begin a counseling session. You feel confident. You have completed the preparation detailed at the beginning of this section. You have reviewed the counseling pitfalls and know to avoid them. Someone will answer your phone. You are ready to listen. Your notes and pencil are in front of you. Your employee walks in. You begin the session.

1. You put the employee at ease by being warm and friendly and using positive body language, lots of eye contact and physically facing the person.

2. You define the reason for the discussion if you called the session, or encourage the employee to define its purpose.

3. You ask open-ended questions about the employee's feelings and thoughts.

4. You paraphrase the content and feelings of the employee's message.

5. You encourage the employee to identify alternatives to solve the problem or resolve the issue.

6. You seek the employee's feelings about the possible consequences of each of the alternatives.

7. You avoid expressing your views but remain alert to provide information on company policies that may help the employee make a decision.

8. You demonstrate empathy for the employee and show confidence in his/her ability to solve problems.

9. You provide support and/or resources when appropriate.

10. You refer to the employee to Human Resources and/or an employee assistance program if the problem is beyond your scope.

11. You summarize key points at the end of the discussion to clarify and seek understanding.

GUIDELINES FOR CONDUCTING A SUCCESSFUL COACHING SESSION

You are ready to begin a coaching session. You feel confident. You have completed the preparation detailed at the beginning of this section. You have reviewed the coaching pitfalls and know you can avoid them. Someone will answer your phone. You are ready to listen. Your notes and pencil are in front of you. Your employee walks in. You begin the session.

1. You put the employee at ease by being warm and friendly.

2. You define the reason for the discussion.

3. You express your concern about the area of performance you feel needs to be improved.

4. You describe the performance problem or area that needs improvement and define its impact on you, the employee, the unit, and the company.

5. You acknowledge and listen to employee's feelings.

6. You seek the employee's opinion on ways to improve performance.

7. You ask open-ended questions to encourage employee's analysis and draw out specific suggestions.

8. You let the employee know that you respect his/her ability to solve problems and develop solutions.

9. You offer suggestions when appropriate, but build on employee's ideas when possible.

10. You agree upon appropriate actions.

11. You schedule a follow-up meeting to ensure accountability and provide feedback on progress (within ten days.)

The session is over. You are relieved and pleased that it went so well. Congratulations!

GUIDELINES FOR CONDUCTING A SUCCESSFUL PERFORMANCE APPRAISAL SESSION

Many managers confuse coaching sessions with performance appraisal* sessions. Performance appraisals will go smoothly if on-going coaching has been provided. At review time, follow the steps below to conduct effective performance appraisal sessions.

1. Put the employee at ease and state the purpose of the meeting—to discuss how they are doing on the job so they can grow professionally and gain clarity about their performance.

2. Engage the employee in the discussion by asking open-ended questions about their self-assessment on each of their goals and/or competencies.

3. Practice active listening skills by showing interest in the employees point of view. Be prepared to change your point of view based on new facts presented by the employee.

4. Discuss strengths and then growth areas for each of their goals and/or competencies. Recognize and reinforce achievements.

5. Express criticism directly and constructively. Discuss problem areas by coaching. Emphasize 2-3 priority areas where improvement is most necessary. Describe how these changes could have greater impact on the employee, team, customer, manager, or business.

6. Seek the employee's opinion on ways they can improve in their growth areas.

7. Ask the employee how you can help them improve in these growth areas.

8. Stay focused on the specifics of the performance appraisal process—do not discuss salary.

9. End on an upbeat note. Thank them for their contribution to the business.

---

*For more information on this topic, read *Effective Performance Appraisals,* 3rd Edition by Robert B. Maddux, Crisp Publications.

WHAT TO DO WHEN ALL ELSE FAILS

Occasionally, despite coaching or counseling sessions, an employee's performance may continue to deteriorate or remain below acceptable standards.

When this happens, you as manager or team leader, must take responsibility for remedying the situation by choosing among the alternatives below. Before determining the best alternative, answer the questions next to each alternative.

Alternatives	Questions to Ask Yourself First
Restructure existing job	1. Does the employee possess enough strength in key areas of the restructured job? 2. Can tasks be eliminated or delegated where employee's performance is below standard?

Transfer to another job within the company	1. Can the employee make a contribution elsewhere in the company?
	
	2. Will a replacement requisition be cut if this person is transferred or terminated, or will I be left with no one to do the job?
	   a. Does the employee have the required intellectual and interpersonal capabilities?
	   b. Is the employee motivated to learn a new job?
	   c. Am I being realistic or simply avoiding responsibility for termination by transferring a "problem" employee to another area?

Disciplinary action and termination	1. Have I given the employee every chance to succeed?
	   a. Has the employee had adequate resources to do the job?
	   b. Has the employee been sufficiently trained and oriented?
	   c. Has the employee been through counseling or coaching sessions?
	
	2. Does the employee understand the expectations and job standards?
	
	3. Has the employee made promises to improve and not kept these promises?
	
	4. Is the individual's performance disrupting the team's performance or affecting business results?

DISCIPLINARY ACTION—
THE LAST ALTERNATIVE

If you have tried your best as a manager to help an employee improve his or her performance and your efforts have not helped, you will need to initiate disciplinary action. Disciplinary action should be reserved for situations when improvement does not occur in a reasonable amount of time, six months to one year, depending on the performance problem. In such cases, discipline should be spelled out in advance, and it should come as a corrective and logical consequence. No surprises or arbitrary actions like ''lowering the boom'' should occur. Even if discipline is used, action plans to improve performance should be developed. This section will help you carry out that action.

Definition

Disciplinary Action: A formal management system designed to get the employee to accept responsibility for his or her own behavior and agree
to improve performance or face specific prescribed alternatives.

1. DOCUMENT EMPLOYEE'S PERFORMANCE

The manager needs to keep an informal file on each employee, recording dates and times of the counseling or coaching sessions. The manager's notes should include what was discussed, what was agreed upon and whether performance problems have improved, stayed the same or deteriorated. Specific and measurable performance objectives should be defined in any disciplinary action plan. Before terminating an employee for poor performance, the manager should have a minimum of six counseling sessions recorded over a minimum period of six weeks.

2. INVOLVE HUMAN RESOURCES OR PERSONNEL

Make sure you are working within your organization's policies when instituting a disciplinary action. Check with your Human Resources or Personnel Manager *before* you move into the ''Required Steps in Disciplinary Action'' shown on the next page.

3. GET YOUR MANAGER'S SUPPORT

Make sure your judgments and decisions are supported by *your* manager. It is wise to keep him or her informed during the disciplinary action process. It is also a good idea to solicit his or her advice and approval.

REQUIRED STEPS IN DISCIPLINARY ACTION

LEVEL 1: VERBAL WARNING

A verbal warning is a conversation between an employee and manager to correct a performance problem by formally bringing it to the attention of the employee. After meeting with the employee, the manager may wish to prepare a memo of the verbal warning for the files. If such a memo is prepared a copy should be given to the employee. Verbal warnings are best given in private.

LEVEL 2: WRITTEN REMINDER

If the employee fails to make the desired performance changes following a verbal warning, a Level 2 action should be taken. A *written reminder* is documentation of a formal discussion between a manager and an employee regarding a performance problem. The discussion is followed by a letter written to the employee, which summarizes the conversation. A copy of this letter is generally sent to Human Resources and put in the employee's file.

LEVEL 3: TERMINATION DISCUSSION

Manager informs the employee that he/she is terminated from the company, giving specific reasons which relate to the Level 2 written reminder. The manager, in conjunction with the Human Resources, is responsible for all termination and severance arrangements.*

Important Information Ahead

---

*For in-depth coverage of this subject, order *Rightful Termination: Avoiding Litigation*, by Ron Visconti and Richard Stiller, Menlo Park, CA: Crisp, 1994.

TERMINATION IN TOUGH SITUATIONS

In order to avoid a wrongful discharge suit against the company, a manager should follow the Required Disciplinary Action Steps listed previously. However, in the following situations, a manager may consider the immediate suspension of the employee. Check your company policy on these situations before taking action.

- Theft of company property

- Intentional damage to company property

- Hostile relationships with customers

- Criminal behavior

- Insubordination

- Any violence or threats of violence by an employee against the life, health, well-being, family or property of others, made while on the company premises, at company functions or in other circumstances, which may have an adverse impact on the company's ability to do business.

WHEN TERMINATING A POTENTIALLY VIOLENT EMPLOYEE

DO NOT

Conduct the discussion if you are the target of the employee's threats or obsessions. Find a Human Resources professional to conduct the session.

Negotiate over anything.

Argue with the employee about the company, management, etc.

Get into specifics about the past bahavior.

Make threats.

Hurt the employee's self-esteem.

Discuss how the employee could have the job.

Use threatening body language.

Promise special severance arrangements.

Allow your own emotions to make you lose control.

TERMINATION (continued)

WHEN TERMINATING A POTENTIALLY VIOLENT EMPLOYEE

DO

Treat the individual with respect and dignity.

Try to stay calm. Rehearse ahead of time and write down what you will say.

Prepare for the worst realistic outcome—just in case. If the potential for violence is high, have internal security personnel nearby or even in the room.

State your understanding of the situation (bizarre behavior, threats, altercations, etc.), based on your investigation.

Keep the discussion short and general, focusing on company policy.

State, ''We have no choice but to (suspend or terminate) you due to unacceptable behavior according to our company policies.''

Let the person know that you think he or she will behave in a professional manner.

Describe the severance arrangements and logistics.

Emphasize the future—that you know he or she can be successful elsewhere.

Collect all company property—keys, access cards, etc. Make sure the termination is complete.

S E C T I O N

V

Pulling It All Together

CASE STUDIES FOR COACHING AND COUNSELING

Develop a coaching and/or counseling plan for each of the following situations and compare your ideas with those of the author on the following page. Include in your plan the type of feedback you will use to motivate the employee.

CASE 1: You have just hired Tara. She is a software engineer who has just graduated from a major university. Although she is a recent graduate, you feel confident that she will bring enthusiasm and fresh ideas to her new job as a programmer. You have given her an important new project to work on.

You would: COACH _____   COUNSEL _____

(Please explain your answer)

_____

_____

_____

_____

_____

_____

_____

_____

_____

(Author's answer on page 77)

CASE 2:

Marsha is a sales manager in your retail firm. She has been with the company five years and seems to love her job. She was promoted last month to sales manager due to her ability to get along well with coworkers, customers and management. You have been swamped and have not had much time to spend with her. She just stopped by to discuss how she feels about her new job. She has stated that she is feeling overwhelmed by all the responsibilities and is unsure of her ability to handle all the pressure.

You would: COACH _____   COUNSEL _____

(Please explain your answer)

_____

_____

_____

_____

_____

_____

_____

_____

_____

_____

(Author's answer of page 77)

CASE 3:

Your boss of the last three years, Fred, stopped by for a chat. He has seemed "out of sorts" lately—depressed and irritable. You genuinely like working for Fred and feel he is an excellent role model for you as a manager. You don't know much about his personal life except that he is a family man and his wife, Mary, is vice president of a large insurance company. Fred has three kids aged six, eight and ten. Fred is now saying that his wife has been offered a job in charge of a new division in Chicago and she really wants to take it. He is very concerned about the problems of relocating. He doesn't want to take the kids out of school. Also, he is a candidate for a promotion. He is having a difficult time trying to decide what to do. Fred asks for your advice.

You would: COACH _____   COUNSEL _____

(Please explain your answer)

_____

_____

_____

_____

_____

_____

_____

_____

_____

_____

(Author's answer on page 77)

CASE 4: Joan, your Production Control Supervisor, has been working for you for three years. She has been your star performer. She has implemented a new PC system, organized the work flow procedures and gets along well with all of the group managers. Unfortunately, a recent downturn in company sales has led to a budget freeze. Although you have an open manager's position, you are currently unable to promote Joan, even though she is your first choice. You know that Joan has a strong future with your company and want her to stay and "weather the current financial crisis." She has called you to set up an appointment to discuss her career options.

You would: COACH _____   COUNSEL _____

(Please explain your answer)

_____

_____

_____

_____

_____

_____

_____

_____

_____

(Author's answer on page 78)

CASE 5: Ned is a Marketing Specialist who is quite ambitious. He's been working for you for three months and you are basically pleased with the work he's done, although you have seen him overstep his boundaries at department meetings. You have had complaints from other team members about how he forces his ideas on others and seldom listens to theirs. He also seems to talk about *his* needs, career goals and strengths constantly. On two occasions you noticed he took credit for the ideas of other team members in front of upper management.

You would: COACH _____   COUNSEL _____

(Please explain your answer)

_____

_____

_____

_____

_____

_____

_____

_____

_____

(Author's answer on page 78)

CASE 6: John has worked for you for the past year. He has been a steady, moderate performer, but lately you have become very concerned about his work. For the past six months you have noticed him coming in late, taking long lunches and leaving early. You have discussed your concerns with him and coached him on the importance of good work habits. He confided in you that he was having marital problems and his wife was seeking a separation. You gave him two weeks to ''sort things out'' but told him you expected him to be punctual and get back on track by then. Four weeks have gone by and his performance has continued to deteriorate. He has become belligerent and hostile and other members of the team have complained about his behavior. One mentioned that John has been drinking excessively every day at lunch.

You would: COACH _____   COUNSEL _____

(Please explain your answer)

_____

_____

_____

_____

_____

_____

_____

_____

(Author's answers on page 78)

AUTHOR'S SUGGESTED ANSWERS TO CASE STUDIES

CASE 1 (page 71)

Answer: **This new employee needs to be coached.** Your coaching plan should include: 1) an orientation to the company, the team and the unit; 2) an initial work plan with realistic goals for the first few months; 3) training on any skills she needs for the job but does not possess; 4) communication of job standards, procedures, goals and rules within the team; 5) consistent supportive feedback in the form of advice and communicative reinforcement of recognizing desired performance.

CASE 2 (page 72)

Answer: **Both counseling and coaching are in order.** Your plan should include: 1) showing Marsha your support and reassurance by listening to her feelings and empathizing with her; 2) sending Marsha to management training class as you cannot assume that she knows how to manage simply because she now has a management title. Being a sales representative is quite different from being a sales manager; 3) coaching Marsha on how to make the transition from being an individual contributor to being a manager.

CASE 3 (page 73)

Answer: **Counseling is in order here,** as the boss has initiated the discussion and it does not involve a performance problem. Your counseling plan should include: 1) empathetic listening; 2) exploration of his feelings and concerns; 3) discussion of all possible alternatives and the consequences of each; 4) letting him know that you believe he can make the best decisions and offering him your continual support during this process.

AUTHOR'S SUGGESTED ANSWER
TO CASE STUDIES (continued)

CASE 4 (page 74)

Answer: **Counseling is the best choice.** Your counseling plan should include:
1) helping Joan explore her interests, values and goals; 2) assisting Joan in matching present opportunities in the company (perhaps you can help her transfer to an area with more mobility); 3) working with Joan to restructure her present job so that she is more challenged; 4) giving Joan opportunities for professional development in her present job, i.e. attending classes or conferences, serving on a special task force, giving presentations to upper management.

CASE 5 (page 75)

Answer: **Coaching is the best choice.** Your coaching plan should include: 1) letting Ned know your expectations in terms of the need for him to build strong relationships with other team members; 2) communicating to him that you will reward collaborative and cooperative behavior, not competitive behavior; 3) determining his career goals and giving him advice about how to achieve his goals; (i.e. tying desired performance to his future career goals. Explain to him the need for interdependence with other people in order to get ahead in the unit and company); 4) reinforcing collaborative and cooperative behavior when he demonstrates it.

CASE 6 (page 76)

Answer: **Counseling and a disciplinary action plan are in order.** Your counseling plan should consist of the following: 1) informing John that you are very concerned about his job performance; 2) asking him to discuss the obstacles to his job performance; 3) describing the impact his performance has on you and the unit; 4) helping him explore alternative solutions to the performance problems; 5) getting a commitment from him to improve performance *immediately*; 6) scheduling a follow-up meeting and give him reinforcement for performance improvement. If performance does not improve and remain consistent, 7) immediately have a Level I disciplinary discussion with him and document all your discussions. Also, inform your manager and check your personnel policy.

PERSONAL ACTION PLAN

Research has shown that if you use a new skill or knowledge right away you are likely to retain the knowledge or skill. Conversely, if you don't use it, you're likely to forget it. It helps to make a commitment to using new knowledge and skills in your professional and personal life.

Think about the information in this book. Review the exercises, questionnaires and case studies. What did you learn about yourself as a counselor? As a coach? Where do you need to improve? Then, develop your personal action plan below.

1. My counseling skills are effective in these areas:

2. My counseling skills need improvement in these areas:

3. My coaching skills are effective in these areas:

4. My coaching skills need improvement in these areas:

5. I will use my improved coaching and counseling skills with the following people on the following dates:

Person _____ Date _____

Person _____ Date _____

Your signature _____ Date: _____

NOTES

NOTES

NOTES

NOTES

NOTES

NOTES

NOW AVAILABLE FROM
CRISP PUBLICATIONS

Books • Videos • CD Roms • Computer-Based Training Products

Subject Areas Include:

Management

Human Resources

Communication Skills

Personal Development

Marketing/Sales

Organizational Development

Customer Service/Quality

Computer Skills

Small Business and Entrepreneurship

Adult Literacy and Learning

Life Planning and Retirement

CRISP WORLDWIDE DISTRIBUTION

English language books are distributed worldwide. Major international distributors include:

ASIA/PACIFIC

Australia/New Zealand: In Learning, PO Box 1051, Springwood QLD, Brisbane, Australia 4127   Tel: 61-7-3-841-2286, Facsimile: 61-7-3-841-1580
ATTN: Messrs. Gordon

Singapore: 85, Genting Lane, Guan Hua Warehouse Bldng #05-01, Singapore 349569   Tel: 65-749-3389, Facsimile: 65-749-1129
ATTN: Evelyn Lee

Japan: Phoenix Associates Co., LTD., Mizuho Bldng. 3-F, 2-12-2, Kami Osaki, Shinagawa-Ku, Tokyo 141   Tel: 81-33-443-7231, Facsimile: 81-33-443-7640
ATTN: Mr. Peter Owans

CANADA

Reid Publishing, Ltd., Box 69559-109 Thomas Street, Oakville, Ontario Canada L6J 7R4.   Tel: (905) 842-4428, Facsimile: (905) 842-9327
ATTN: Mr. Stanley Reid

Trade Book Stores: *Raincoast Books,* 8680 Cambie Street, Vancouver, B.C., V6P 6M9   Tel: (604) 323-7100, Facsimile: (604) 323-2600
ATTN: Order Desk

EUROPEAN UNION

England: *Flex Training,* Ltd. 9-15 Hitchin Street, Baldock, Hertfordshire, SG7 6A, England   Tel: 44-1-46-289-6000, Facsimile: 44-1-46-289-2417
ATTN: Mr. David Willetts

INDIA

Multi-Media HRD, Pvt., Ltd., National House, Tulloch Road, Appolo Bunder, Bombay, India 400-039   Tel: 91-22-204-2281, Facsimile: 91-22-283-6478
ATTN: Messrs. Aggarwal

SOUTH AMERICA

Mexico: *Grupo Editorial Iberoamerica,* Nebraska 199, Col. Napoles, 03810 Mexico, D.F.   Tel: 525-523-0994, Facsimile: 525-543-1173
ATTN: Señor Nicholas Grepe

SOUTH AFRICA

Alternative Books, Unit A3 Micro Industrial Park, Hammer Avenue, Stridom Park, Randburg, 2194 South Africa   Tel: 27-11-792-7730, Facsimile: 27-11-792-7787
ATTN: Mr. Vernon de Haas